# COLORS OF THE GRITTIEST GOD

An Intertwining Collaboration

Karla Van Vliet
Kristine Snodgrass

Other Books by Karla Van Vliet:
She Speaks Tongues: poems || asemic writing
Fluency: A Collection of Asemic Writing
The River From My Mouth
From the Book of Remembrance

Chapbooks:
Fragments: From the Lost Book of the Bird Spirit
Wildwood Devotions: poems || asemics
Bone Scribed: poems || asemics


Other Books by Kristine Snodgrass:
Robot, Girl
Neon Galax (with Andrew Brenza)
Rank
American Apparell
Whistle (with De Villo Sloan)
Out of the World
The War on Pants
Two Thieves & a Liar: Poems in Collaboration
with Neil de la Flor and Maureen Seaton

Chapbooks
Zero-Zero w Maureen Seaton
Rather, (Contagion Press 2020)
These Burning Fields
Fledgling Starlet
Ho in a Dream
Put the Pie Away Quietly and Without Fervor
Facial Geometry by Neil de la Flor,
Maureen Seaton & Kristine Snodgrass
Hot Body Contest (with Scott Sweeney)

# COLORS OF THE GRITTIEST GOD

An Intertwining Collaboration

Karla Van Vliet
Kristine Snodgrass

Hysterical Books

# Colors of the Gritiest God



Published by Hysterical Books, 2024
Interior and cover design by Karla Van Vliet

Cover image: Karla Van Vliet, Kristine Snodgrass


Hysterical Books




Printed in the United States of America

ISBN: 978-0-940821-26-2 (softcover)

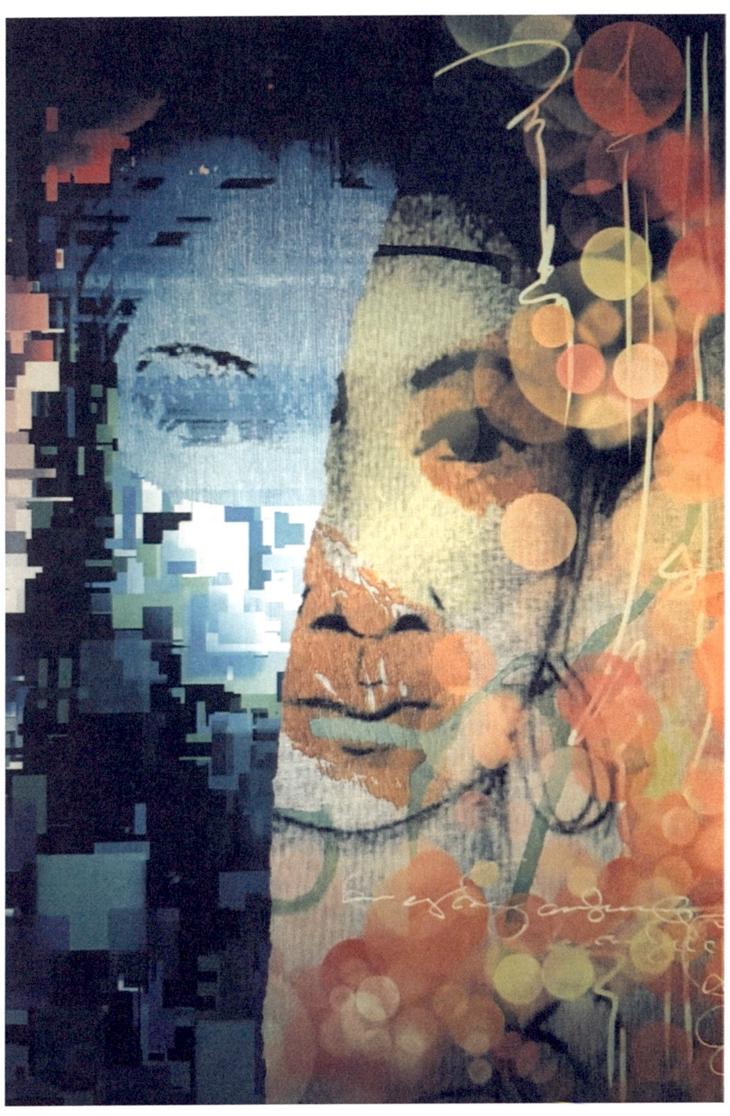

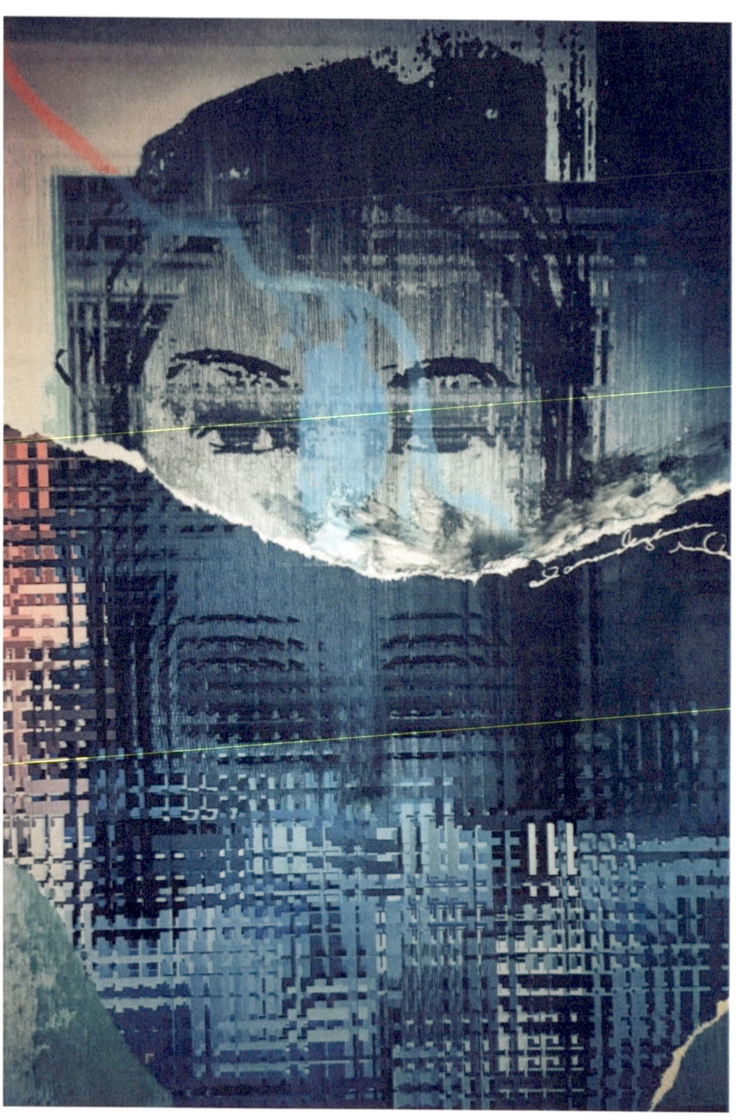

I

Hunger-lives

     loves fruit slowly garden's

             cellblock

*chop chop chop*

       wing sliced sky

    rued rainfall

       weeping empties the body

II

swinging up fragrance

                  to allow

low and ebbing

     touch

        yours


sensation a scent

     these thin white blossoms


        covering the lattice

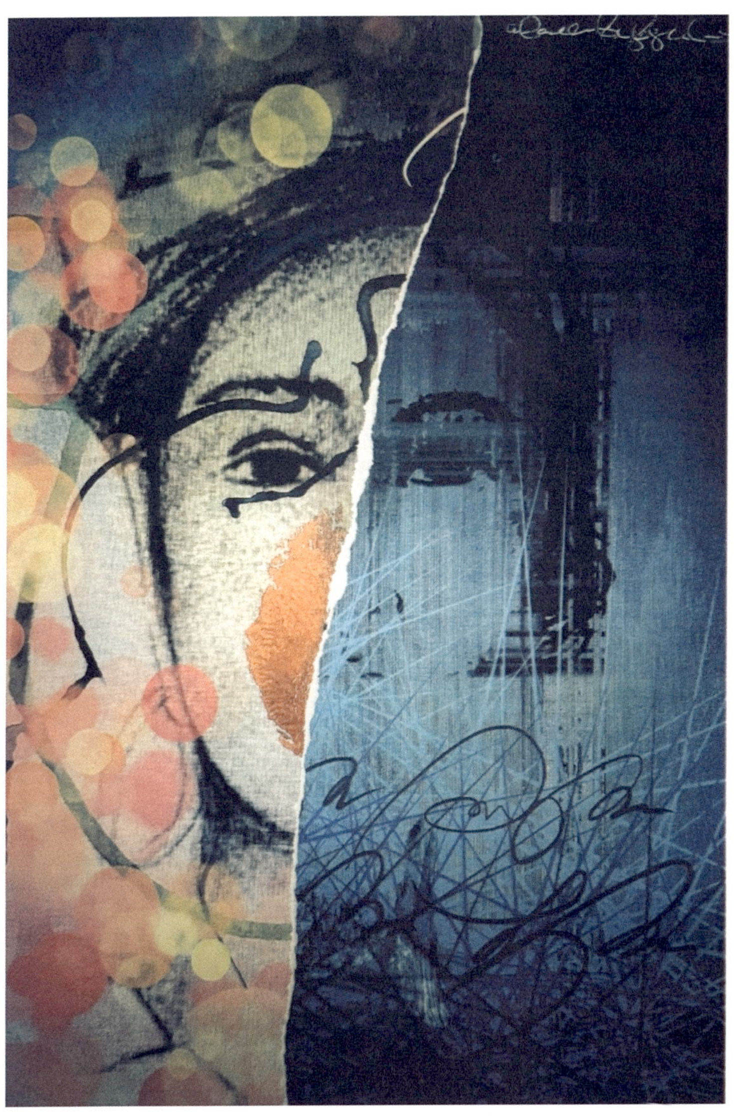

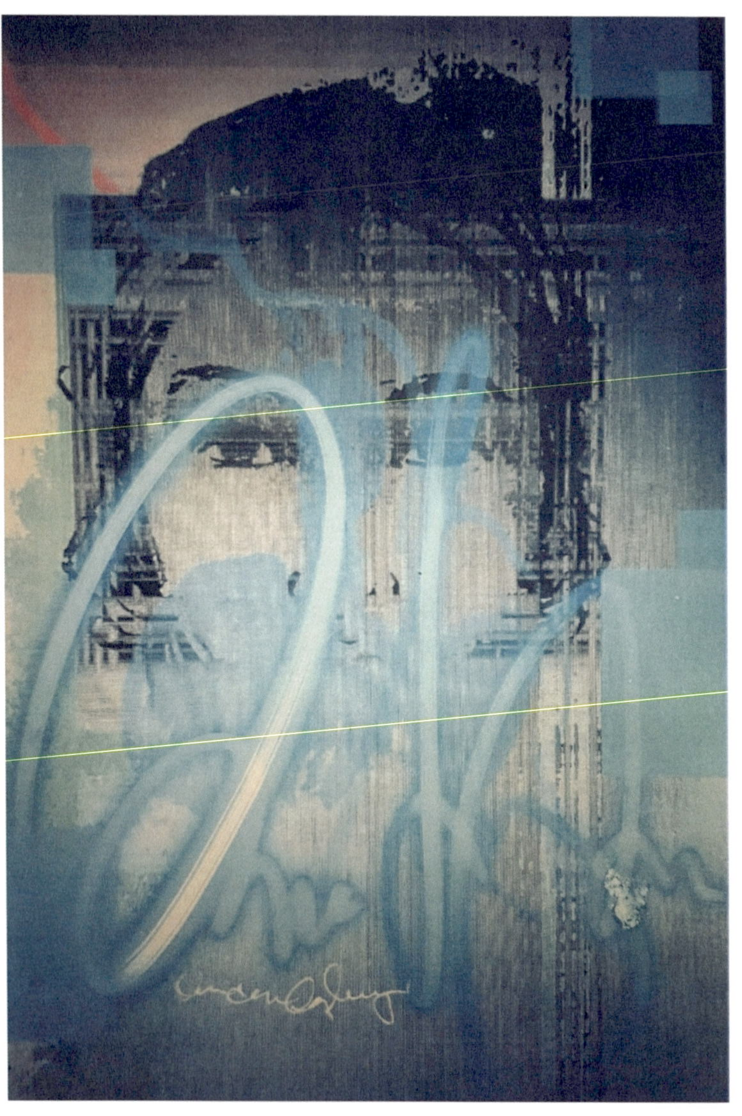

III

a bustle in the public garden

       a violet tormented, says

*fight*

    says *my body*

       says   *let the tender be*


*fierce*

IV


divides duration

        clouds failing   and ground

  swells


         there is only a screen

or shadow
          brought wild



   a storm       plundered sky

demanding

     change

   the tree the tree


             downed

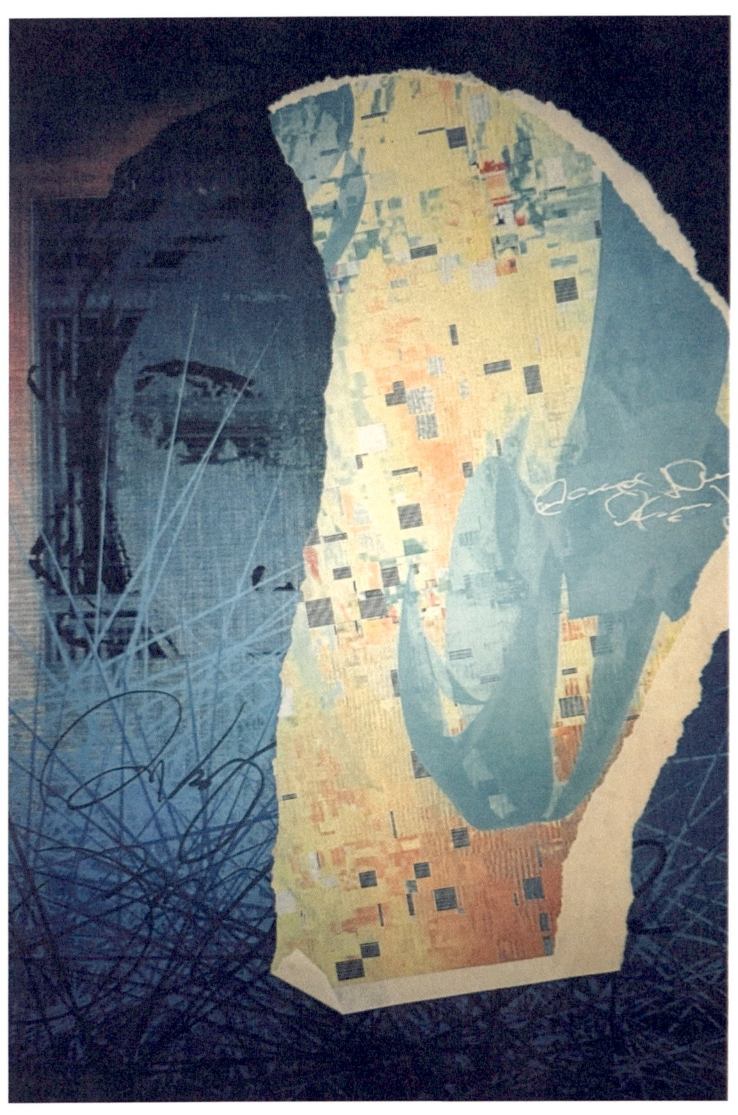

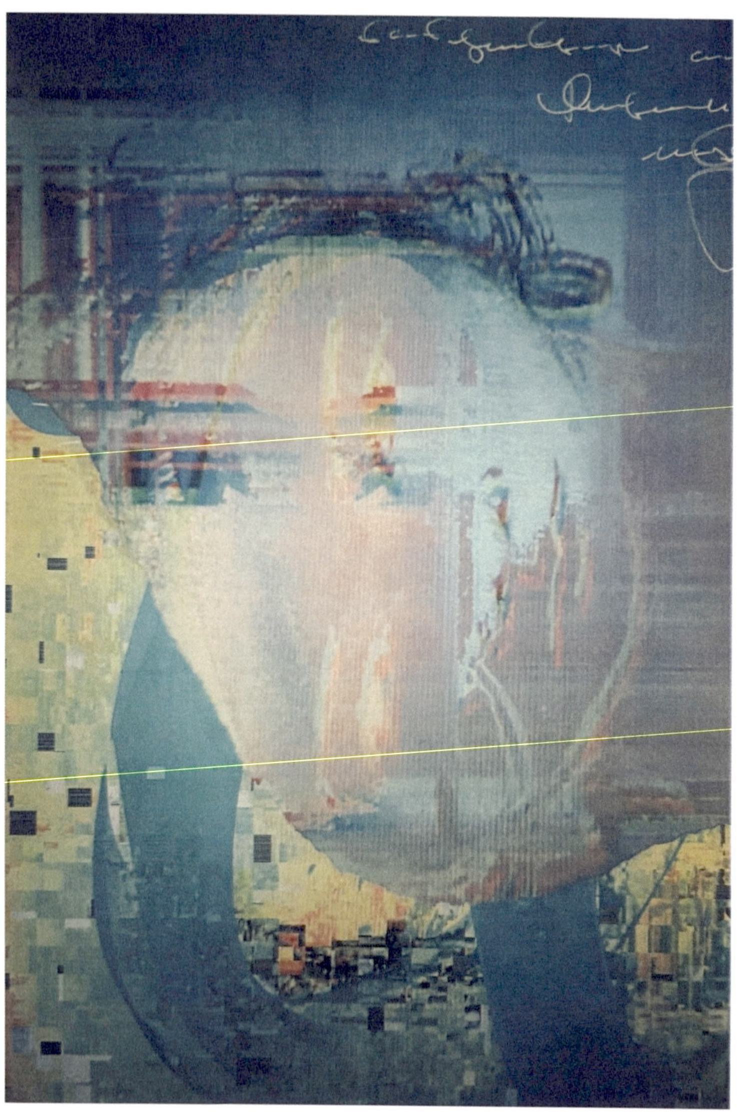

V

520 degrees

                together no hindrance that

rides


listless      certain dancing

                        they carve it up

    put it in the street


            the white flag

                        on fire


        the grandmothers are rising

the damned    be damned

                    nothing to lose

VI

       they played the piano

and plagues of the body

          and burners

       like unbelievable hunting


grinding stone into her lap

          like that

       *Colors of the Grittiest God...*

like tears
                    chaff
     the notes
               spill




crimson   vermilion   scarlet


                         sanguine


               spit blood

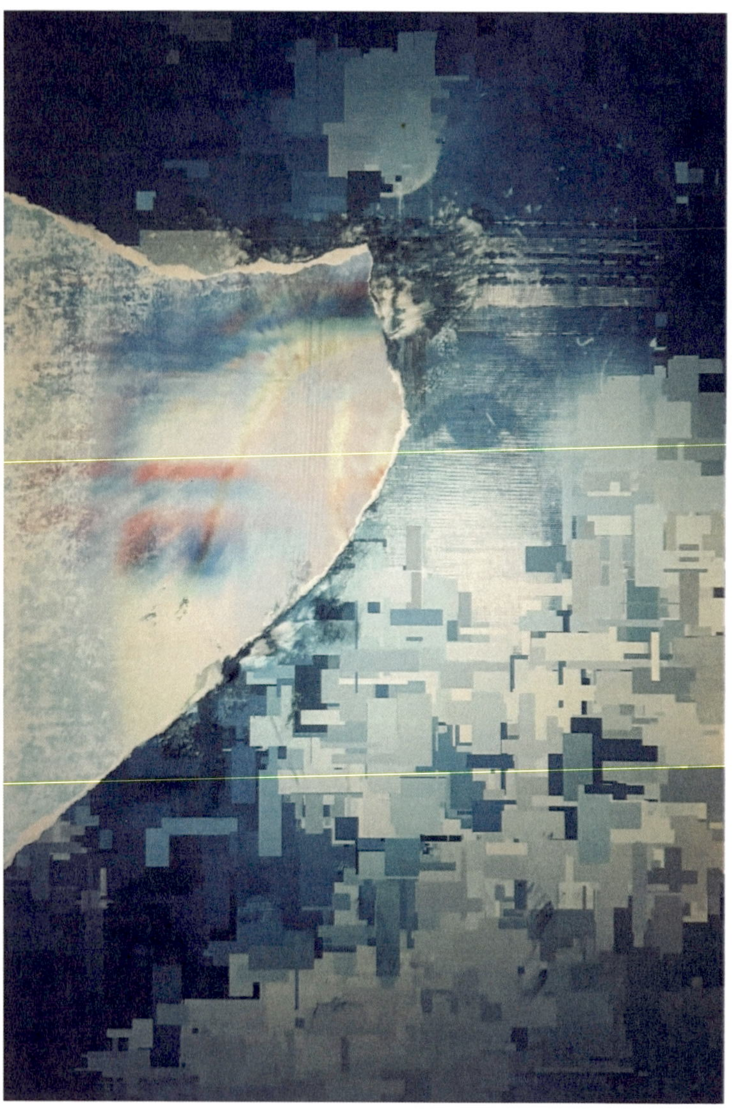

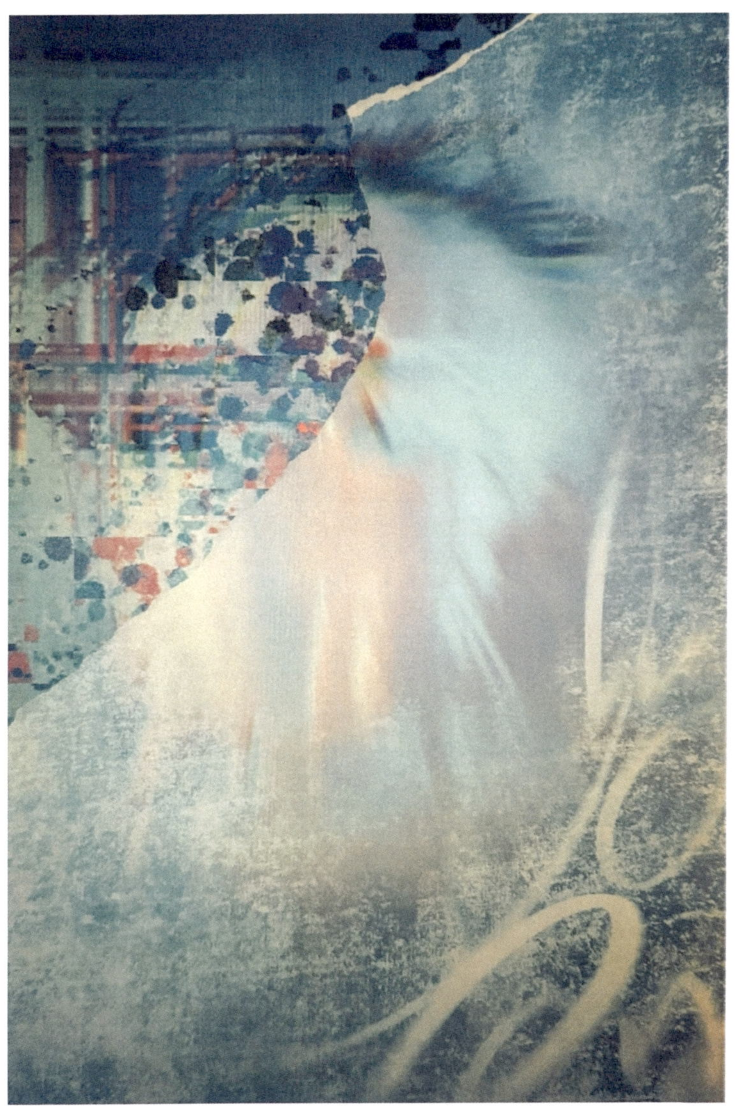

VII

turquoise saint at the window

          like a star vowing (to render)

                         there is a noble velvet

                                      in this way

the inside of found cheeks

          she says

                *God's immortal brew*

taste of ground

blue

sky rain mud

in her hands

fingers mold   roundelay

sing

*her flesh*

*her flesh*        *her flesh*

until what is uttered is held in hand

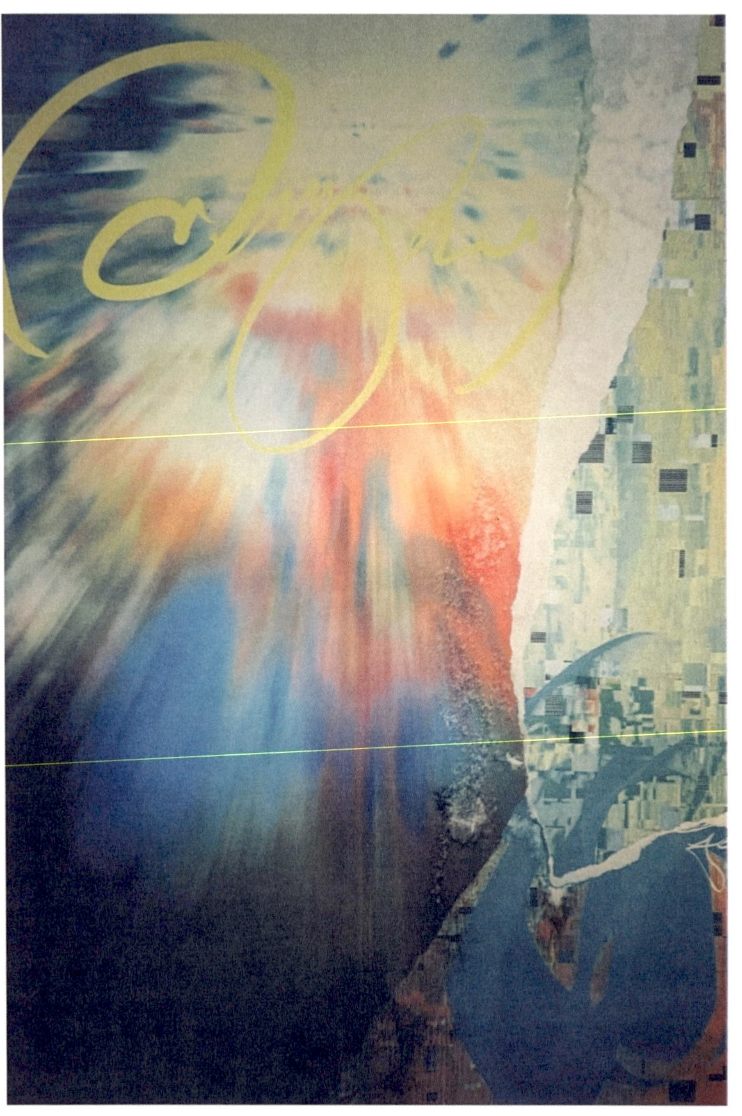

www.ingramcontent.com/pod-product-compliance
Lightning Source LLC
Chambersburg PA
CBRC091240050726
47599CB00008B/953